INSPIRATIONAL LIVES

MO FARAH

OLYMPIC HERO

Simon Hart

WAYLAND

First published in 2013 by Wayland

Copyright © Wayland 2013

Wayland
338 Euston Road
London NW1 3BH

Wayland Australia
Level 17/207 Kent Street
Sydney, NSW 2000

Editor: Nicola Edwards
Design: Basement68

A catalogue record for this book is
available from the British Library.

ISBN: 978 0 7502 7996 3

Printed in China

Wayland is a division of
Hachette Children's Books,
an Hachette UK company.

www.hachette.co.uk

Picture acknowledgements:
The author and publisher would like
to thank the following for allowing
their pictures to be reproduced in
this publication:
Cover: Martin Rickett/PA Wire; pp4, 5
Mike King; p6 Sayyid Azim/AP/Press
Association Images; p7 PIERRE-PHILIPPE
MARCOU/AFP/Getty Images; p8 Arsenal
FC via Getty Images; p9 Getty Images for
Aviva; pp10, 11, 12, 13 Mark Shearman –
Athletics Images; p14 AP Photo/Fabrizio
Giovannozzi; p15 Antonio Calanni/AP/
Press Association Images; p16 Mark
Baker/AP/Press Association Images; p17
AP Photo/Thomas Kienzle; p18 David
Davies/PA Archive/Press Association
Images; p19 Anja Niedringhaus/AP/
Press Association Images; p20 Sports
Illustrated/Getty Images; p21 Adam Davy/
EMPICS Sport; p22 Mike King; p23 Adam
Davy/PA Wire; p24 Martin Rickett/PA
Wire; p25 AFP/Getty Images; p26 Martin
Rickett/PA Wire; p27 Mike King; p28 John
Stillwell/PA Wire; p29 Sean Dempsey/PA
Wire

Contents

Mighty Mo

In the space of one amazing week in 2012, Mo Farah made history by winning two long-distance running gold medals at the London Olympics. First, he won the 10,000 metres race and then, seven days later, he triumphed in the 5,000 metres. His two victories turned him into an instant Olympic hero and proved that he is Britain's greatest-ever male long-distance runner.

Mo was born in Somalia in east Africa and moved to Britain when he was eight. His talent for running was obvious from an early age and he went on to win five English Schools titles. His success continued when he became a **professional** athlete.

In 2010 he became the first British runner to win gold medals over 5,000 and 10,000 metres at the European Championships. A year later, he showed he was one of the best athletes in the world when he won a 5,000 metres gold medal and 10,000 metres silver at the World Championships.

Mo takes the lead in the 5,000 metres final in London, on his way to Olympic gold.

INSPIRATION

'I hope I inspire the next generation and teach them hard work and dedication.' – Mo Farah

The London Olympics were Mo's crowning glory. Roared on by 80,000 spectators in the Olympic Stadium, Mo sprinted away from his rivals to win gold in the 10,000 metres final with several metres to spare. The crowd went wild.

After the race, Mo admitted he was exhausted by the effort and many people thought it would not be possible for him to win another gold a week later. But Mo was not finished. In a thrilling 5,000 metres final, he made it a double Olympic triumph on a night of sport that few will forget.

A delighted Mo celebrates victory with his now-famous 'Mobot' pose, placing his hands on top of his head in the shape of an 'M' for Mo.

HONOURS BOARD

Mo's medals

London Olympics 2012
Gold: 10,000 metres
Gold: 5,000 metres

World Championships
2011 (Daegu)
Silver: 10,000 metres
Gold: 5,000 metres

European Indoor Championships
2011 (Paris)
Gold: 3,000 metres

European Championships
2010 (Barcelona)
Gold: 10,000 metres
Gold: 5,000 metres

European Indoor Championships
2009 (Turin)
Gold: 3,000 metres

European Championships
2006 (Gothenburg)
Silver: 5,000 metres

Growing up in Africa

Mohamed Farah, or 'Mo' as he is better known, was born in Mogadishu, in the east African country of Somalia, on March 23rd, 1983. He has an identical twin brother, Hassan, two other brothers and two sisters.

When Mo was a small child he lived with father, Muktar, his mother, Amran, and the rest of his family in a comfortable stone house in Mogadishu. But when **civil war** broke out in Somalia, the family was forced to leave. The city was too violent and dangerous for young children.

The family moved to Somaliland, in the north of Somalia, but life was very difficult there so they moved again to the neighbouring country of Djibouti to stay with Mo's grandmother. To try to earn money for the family, Muktar flew to London, where he had lived and worked before he was married.

WOW!

While Mo's family were in Somaliland they had to live in a small tent in a refugee camp. There was no electricity and very little food.

A tank rolling down a street was a common sight in the Somalian capital of Mogadishu during the civil war. Mo's family fled the country to escape the violence.

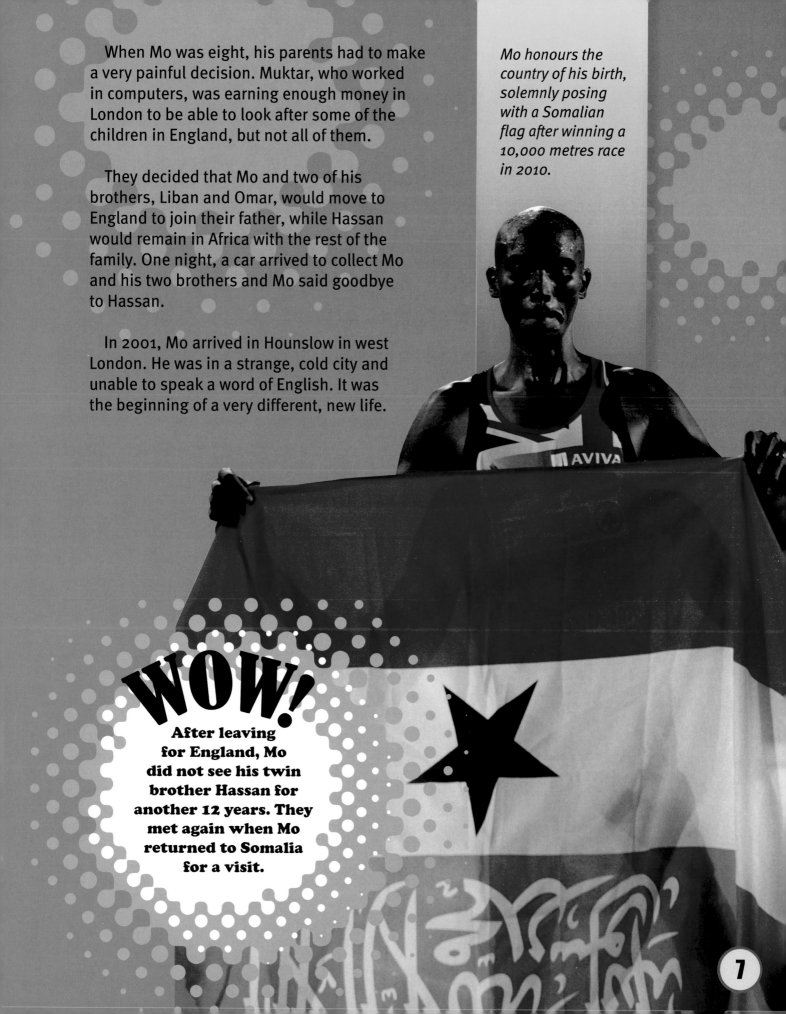

When Mo was eight, his parents had to make a very painful decision. Muktar, who worked in computers, was earning enough money in London to be able to look after some of the children in England, but not all of them.

They decided that Mo and two of his brothers, Liban and Omar, would move to England to join their father, while Hassan would remain in Africa with the rest of the family. One night, a car arrived to collect Mo and his two brothers and Mo said goodbye to Hassan.

In 2001, Mo arrived in Hounslow in west London. He was in a strange, cold city and unable to speak a word of English. It was the beginning of a very different, new life.

Mo honours the country of his birth, solemnly posing with a Somalian flag after winning a 10,000 metres race in 2010.

WOW!

After leaving for England, Mo did not see his twin brother Hassan for another 12 years. They met again when Mo returned to Somalia for a visit.

A new start

Mo had a tough introduction to life in England. He started as a pupil at Oriel Junior School but he could not speak any English, which made it difficult to fit in. He loved messing about and having fun but he often got into trouble with his teachers. By the time he started senior school, his grasp of the English language was still very poor.

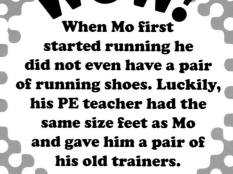

WOW!

When Mo first started running he did not even have a pair of running shoes. Luckily, his PE teacher had the same size feet as Mo and gave him a pair of his old trainers.

There was one thing Mo loved more than anything, and you did not need to speak good English to understand it. He adored football, especially Arsenal Football Club. He dreamed about being a professional player.

Mo was spotted playing football by his PE teacher, Alan Watkinson. He was amazed how Mo could run around the pitch without getting out of breath. Mr Watkinson suggested to Mo that he should try athletics.

Mo shows his gold medals and one of his twin babies to the crowd at his beloved Arsenal Football Club.

At first Mo was reluctant to try athletics because he was more interested in football. Mr Watkinson persuaded Mo by promising him that he could have an extra game of football in the school gym if he practised his running.

Mo's talent for athletics was clear when he won the school **cross-country** trials. He was entered for the Hounslow Borough Championships and finished second, but only because he did not know the route of the race. His next challenge was the county championships, and he finished fourth despite slipping over at the start of the race.

Encouraged by Mr Watkinson, Mo took part in other races and began to enjoy athletics more and more. Slowly, his command of English began to improve as well.

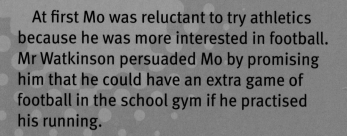

INSPIRATION

'If I had any problem I could go to Alan Watkinson with it after work. He became like a father figure to me. Even now I call him Sir. He's an inspiration.' – Mo Farah.

Alan Watkinson (right) receives a 'School Sport Teacher of the Year' award from Niels de Vos, the chief executive of UK Athletics.

Schoolboy champion

In 1996, Mo competed in the junior boys' race at the English Schools Cross Country Championships. He finished ninth but he was still only 13, which was a year younger than most of his opponents. He was selected as first reserve for the England Schools team.

The following year, Mr Watkinson promised Mo a special prize if he won the English Schools title: a new Arsenal kit. The race was held in Newark, Nottinghamshire, but started badly for Mo when he tripped over. After one kilometre, Mo was in about 20th place but gradually he overtook the other runners until he finally reached the front. He won the race and Mr Watkinson kept his promise about the kit.

It was to be the first of five English Schools titles for Mo in cross-country and track races. By now, Mo was taking his athletics very seriously and was training at Hounslow Athletics Club in his spare time.

INSPIRATION

'It's really important that kids get more active. We need to point them in the right direction, like my PE teacher did for me.' – Mo Farah.

At the age of 14, Mo was already showing his running talent after winning the English Schools Cross Country title.

Because of his success in England Schools races, Mo was selected to run for Great Britain. The problem was that, at that time, Mo was not a full British citizen and did not qualify for a British passport. It made travelling abroad for international races very difficult. Mr Watkinson often had to queue for hours in **embassies** to get Mo a **visa** to travel overseas.

Fortunately Sir Eddie Kulukundis, a very wealthy businessman who loved athletics, had heard about Mo's situation. He offered to pay for legal work to help Mo become a British citizen. Eventually, Mo's British passport arrived and he could now compete in international races without any problems.

WOW!

Paula Radcliffe, the **marathon** world record-holder, paid for Mo to have driving lessons when he was 17 so that he could get to training.

His hairstyle may have changed but there was no mistaking Mo's consistent running ability when he competed at Crystal Palace in 1999, aged 16.

Learning his craft

Mo enjoyed great success competing against other countries in junior cross-country and track races. In 2001, when he was 18, he was presented with his first international title when he won the 5,000 metres gold medal at the European Junior Championships in Grosseto, Italy.

Mo had finished school a few months earlier and was undecided about his future. He was thinking about joining the Army but then he was offered the perfect opportunity to continue his athletics training.

The London Marathon charity was keen to help promising British runners and it agreed to pay for Mo to live and train at a new training centre that had opened recently at St Mary's College in Twickenham, south-west London.

Aged 18, Mo finds himself in a familiar position at the front of the field, during a cross-country race in Margate in 2001.

INSPIRATION

Mo says he is inspired by his Muslim faith. 'It says in the Qur'an that you must work hard in whatever you do, so I work hard in training and that's got a lot to do with being successful,' he says.

One of the **coaches** at St Mary's was Alan Storey. He was an expert in long-distance running and had helped several leading athletes to win Olympic medals. Mo was highly successful as a junior but he needed to learn how to compete as senior athlete, and so Alan took charge of his training.

Mo loved it at St Mary's and ended up staying there for four years. Although he worked hard on the training track, there was also time for fun. He enjoyed being around other athletes, and sometimes they would get up to pranks.

On one occasion, during a night out in nearby Kingston, one of Mo's friends dared him to take off his clothes and jump off Kingston Bridge into the River Thames. Amazingly, Mo did it. It was not kind of behaviour you would expect from a serious athlete, but Mo was still young and determined to enjoy life.

TOP TIP

'Don't wear new trainers for a race. If you're not used to them you could get blisters and you might not be able to finish the race.'
– Mo Farah

Away from athletics, when Mo was 18 he worked in a sports shop to earn some extra money. In 2012 a post box opposite the shop was painted gold to celebrate Mo's Olympic wins.

13

Time to get serious

By the time Farah left St Mary's in 2005 he had already won two silver medals in the 5,000 metres at the European Under-23 Championships. But some people questioned whether he had the right attitude to become a world-beating senior athlete. They wondered whether he was too fond of having fun.

Ricky Simms had become Mo's **agent** to help organise his races. Ricky also worked with several highly successful runners from east Africa who spent part of the year in London, living together in the same house. Ricky suggested that Mo should move in with them to learn how experienced athletes lived.

Mo is beaten to the line by Spain's Jesús España in a 3,000 metres race at the European Cup in Florence, Italy in 2005.

Mo's experience in the house made a big impression on him. He saw how **dedicated** the African runners were. There were no nights out. They just ate simple food, trained and slept, getting up at six in the morning for their first run of the day. It made Mo realise what he had to do if he wanted to be a successful runner like them.

TOP TIP

'It's important that you ease down in the week before your competition because you're not going to get quicker by training hard a week before your race.' – Mo Farah

In 2006, Mo had his first experience of a major senior championship when he travelled to Melbourne, Australia, to compete for England at the Commonwealth Games. Racing against some top African runners, he finished ninth in the 5,000 metres final.

Later that year, Mo had a big breakthrough. At the European Championships in Gothenburg, Sweden, he won his first senior medal when he finished second in the 5,000 metres final. He missed the gold by just half a second.

Mo ended 2006 by winning his first senior gold medal when he triumphed at the European Cross Country Championships in San Giorgio su Legnano, Italy.

Mo celebrates after winning the European Cross Country title in Italy in 2006.

Tough at the top

Many of the world's best long-distance runners come from east Africa. After training with some of them in London, Mo decided to go one step further. In early 2007 he travelled to Kenya for a training camp. The high **altitude** was perfect for fitness work and he learned more about the dedicated lifestyle of the top athletes.

In the summer, Mo competed at his first World Championships. They were held in Osaka, Japan, and Mo did very well to finish in sixth place in the 5,000 metres final.

In May 2008, Mo ran his first ever 10,000 metres and recorded the quickest time by a British athlete for nearly eight years. It showed he was in great physical shape as he prepared for his first Olympic Games in Beijing, China, later that summer.

Mo stumbles during the 5,000 metres at the 2007 World Championships. He still managed to finish the race in sixth place.

WOW!

During the 2007 European Indoor Championships, Mo fell over during his 3,000 metres race. He was so dazed that, after picking himself up, he set off in the opposite direction, back towards the start!

Unfortunately for Mo, the Olympics went disastrously wrong. He ran so poorly that he did not even qualify for the final. It made him realise he would have to train even harder if he wanted to beat the world's leading athletes.

After two training camps in Ethiopia and in Kenya's Rift Valley, Mo was in better **form** at the start of 2009. He broke the British indoor 3,000 metres record twice and then won gold in the 3,000 metres at the European Indoor Championships in Turin, Italy.

In the summer of 2009 he took part in the World Championships in Berlin, Germany, and finished seventh in the 5,000 metres final. His performance was a big improvement on the Olympics but he still needed to be quicker if he wanted to be the best.

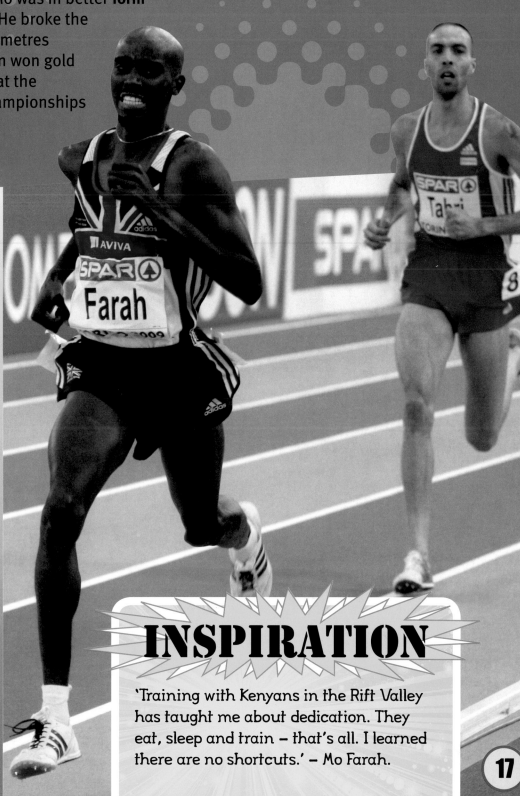

A big breakthrough for Mo as he wins his first senior international title on the track – a gold medal in the 3,000 metres at the European Indoor Championships in Turin, Italy in 2009.

INSPIRATION

'Training with Kenyans in the Rift Valley has taught me about dedication. They eat, sleep and train – that's all. I learned there are no shortcuts.' – Mo Farah.

Getting faster

In April 2010, Mo married Tania Nell. He had known Tania since school and in the last couple of years their friendship had grown into a romance. Tania had a five-year-old daughter, Rihanna, from a previous relationship and so Mo now had a ready-made family to look after.

After the wedding, Mo and Tania went on honeymoon to Zanzibar, Tanzania, but on their way home they got stuck at Nairobi airport. A volcano had erupted in Iceland causing a huge cloud of ash, and grounding all flights.

Instead of waiting with Tania for a flight home, the couple agreed that it would be better if Mo headed straight to his African training camp while Tania returned to Britain on her own. The newly-weds were separated for six weeks. Being a world-class athlete meant lots of sacrifices.

INSPIRATION

Mo showed his gratitude to his old PE teacher, Alan Watkinson, by making him the best man at his wedding. "The person I owe most to is Alan Watkinson," says Mo.

Arriving at an awards ceremony in 2011, Mo poses for a photo on the red carpet with his wife, Tania and daughter, Rihanna.

Mo's dedication to his training paid off a few months later when he travelled to Barcelona, Spain, for the European Championships. Mo was in the best form of his life as he became the first British athlete to win European gold medals in both the 10,000 and 5,000 metres. He was so overcome with emotion after his 5,000 metres win that he broke down in tears.

Mo still had one more thing to achieve before the 2010 season was over. A week after his double triumph, he competed in a 5,000 metres race in Zurich, Switzerland, and became the first British man in history to complete the distance in under 13 minutes.

WOW!

After his double victory in Barcelona, Mo was a guest of honour at Arsenal Football Club. He went on to the pitch at half-time to wave to the crowd but the best bit of the day was watching Arsenal beat Blackpool 6-0!

Mo cries tears of joy after winning the 5,000 metres gold at the 2010 European Championships in Barcelona, Spain, beating his Spanish rival, Jesús España (see page 14).

On top of the world

Mo's two gold medals in Barcelona proved that he was getting quicker and stronger, but he was still only the champion of Europe. To be champion of the entire world was a different matter. Mo decided to make a drastic change in his life to try to achieve it.

In early 2011, Mo announced that he was leaving his old St Mary's coach, Alan Storey, and moving with his family to the United States to train with American coach, Alberto Salazar. They would be based in Portland, Oregon.

At the time, Alberto coached only American runners and was well known for his scientific training techniques. Mo arrived in Portland in March and was immediately given a new training programme. One of Mo's new training methods was running on an underwater treadmill, which allows athletes to build up their **endurance** without any risk of injury.

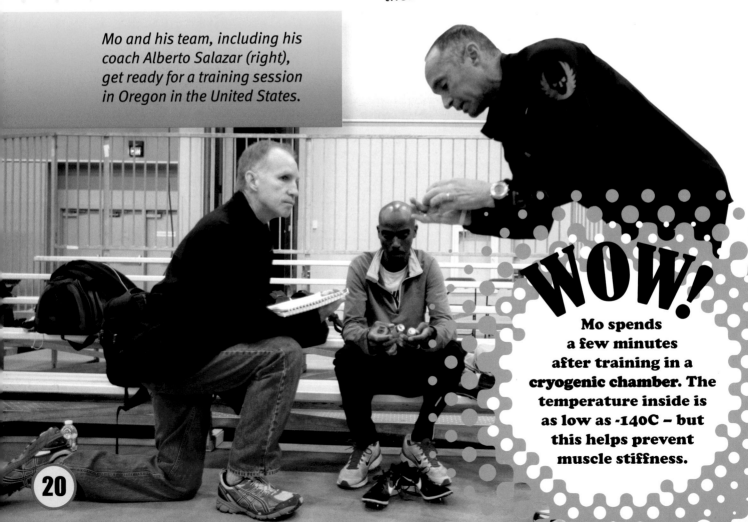

Mo and his team, including his coach Alberto Salazar (right), get ready for a training session in Oregon in the United States.

WOW!

Mo spends a few minutes after training in a cryogenic chamber. The temperature inside is as low as -140C – but this helps prevent muscle stiffness.

The new methods appeared to be working when Mo set a British and European 10,000 metres record in a race in Eugene, Oregon, in June, 2011.

When it came to the World Championships in Daegu, South Korea, later that summer, Mo was in brilliant form. He began the championships by winning the silver medal in the 10,000 metres and ended them with a thrilling gold medal in the 5,000 metres.

Mo's decision to move to America to work with Alberto had paid off. At long last, he was a world-beater. His next mission was to become an Olympic champion as well.

Mo shows he is the best in the world, winning a gold medal in the 5,000 metres at the 2011 World Championships in Daegu, South Korea.

INSPIRATION

After Mo won the world title, a pop song was released in his birth country of Somalia to honour his achievement. The words of the song included the line: "England is proud of you, and we are proud of you too."

Olympic hero

Mo's gold and silver medals at the World Championships meant he was now one of the stars of the British athletics team. He was also one of the favourites to win gold at the 2012 London Olympics.

Mo's first Olympic race was the 10,000 metres on Saturday, August 4th, 2012. The crowd in the stadium was already in a frenzy of excitement before Mo went to the start-line because fellow British athletes Jessica Ennis and Greg Rutherford had already won gold medals.

The noise throughout the race was deafening, and Mo responded to their cheers. In a thrilling final lap, he proved far too quick for his rivals and sprinted away to win the gold.

With arms outstretched and a joyfully amazed expression, Mo is first to cross the finish line in the Olympic final of the 5,000 metres – winning him his second gold of the Games.

HONOURS BOARD

London Olympics, 2012:

10,000 metres
1, Mo Farah (Great Britain)
27 minutes, 30.42 seconds
2, Galen Rupp (United States)
27-30.90
3, Tariku Bekele (Ethiopia)
27-31.43

5,000 metres
1, Mo Farah (Great Britain)
13-41.66
2, Dejen Gebremeskel (Ethiopia)
13-41.98
3, Thomas Longosiwa (Kenya)
13-42.36

The 10,000 m was a **gruelling** race for Mo, and he had just seven days to recover before the final of the 5,000 m. Many people wondered whether he could really win a second Olympic gold.

They need not have worried. In another amazing race, Mo proved himself to be one of the greatest runners of all time by winning the 5,000 m gold. He was only the seventh man in history to achieve the Olympic 5,000-10,000 double.

Jamaican sprint star Usain Bolt was also racing in the Olympic Stadium that evening, and after winning gold in the 4x100 m relay he did the 'Mobot' as well to honour Mo's achievements.

Mo repaid the compliment by performing Usain's famous 'Lightning Bolt' pose. The two athletes celebrated together, both of them Olympic heroes.

HONOURS BOARD

Men who have achieved the 5,000-10,000 metres double at the Olympics

1912: Hannes Kolehmainen (Finland)
1952: Emil Zatopek (Czechoslovakia)
1956: Vladimir Kuts (Soviet Union)
1972 & 1976: Lasse Viren (Finland)
1980: Miruts Yifter (Ethiopia)
2008: Kenenisa Bekele (Ethiopia
2012: Mo Farah (Great Britain)

Mo and Jamaican sprint champion Usain Bolt swap their trademark 'Mobot' and 'Lightning Bolt' poses on the podium at the London Olympics.

Twin celebrations

Not long after winning his two Olympic gold medals, Mo had another double celebration. On August 24th, 2012, Tania gave birth to twin daughters, Aisha and Amani. Mo said that each girl would be given one of his gold medals with her name engraved on it.

As a twin himself, Mo's thoughts turned to his brother, Hassan, who had remained behind in Africa when Mo moved to London as an eight-year-old. Although Mo had seen Hassan a few times on visits to Somalia, he had never spoken publicly about his brother. When a newspaper reporter travelled to Somalia and tracked Hassan down, Mo finally decided to tell the story of how they had been separated.

Hassan had never been to England before, so Mo put that right by inviting his brother to London for a visit to join in the family celebrations. Rihanna joked that the two brothers looked just the same except that Hassan was a bit fatter. Hassan still lives in Somalia with his own family and has a comfortable life working as a telephone engineer.

The day after his victory in the 5,000 metres, Mo proudly shows off the two gold medals he won at the 2012 Olympic Games.

Mo's Olympic achievements turned him into a celebrity. His 'Mobot' celebration also turned into a national craze. All over the country, people were putting their hands on their heads in the shape of an 'M'.

Towards the end of the year, Mo was given official recognition when the Queen appointed him a Commander of the British Empire (CBE). It was quite an honour for the man who had arrived in London as a child unable to speak any English and with a habit of getting into trouble. It showed what can be achieved with dedication and hard work.

WOW!

When Mo won the 5,000 metres, the noise in the stadium reached 140 decibels (as loud as a plane's jet engine). It made the camera on the finish line start to shake!

Mo's 'Mobot' celebration became so popular that even Prince Charles was pictured doing it at an awards ceremony after the Olympics.

WOW!

Mo Farah is the British record-holder for the 5,000 metres, 10,000 metres and half-marathon. He plans to compete in the full marathon in the future.

A day in the life of Mo Farah

At home in America, Mo usually wakes up at 7am and has a breakfast of black coffee and porridge or toast. Training begins at 8.30am with a running session at the Nike Centre in Portland. Mo's training varies from day to day but usually his coach, Alberto Salazar, is there to watch him. Twice a week, Mo goes to the gym for some weight training.

Mo often trains with the American runner, Galen Rupp. He is also a world-class athlete and finished second behind Mo in the Olympic 10,000 metres final in London to earn the silver medal. The two men are firm friends.

After the morning session, Mo goes home for a quick nap before lunch. He normally eats a tuna sandwich or some chicken. The food is low in fat but high in **protein** and **carbohydrates**. Protein helps his muscles recover from hard running sessions while carbohydrates give Mo energy.

American athlete Galen Rupp trains with Mo in Portland, Oregon, and won the Olympic silver medal behind Mo in the 10,000 metres in London.

INSPIRATION

'I train hard. Anything is possible. You just have to work hard at what you do and that's the secret.' – Mo Farah

Three times a week, Mo goes for a sports massage in the afternoon. Sometimes he also sees a **sports psychologist** to help him prepare mentally for races.

At 5 o'clock, Mo has his second run of the day, which is usually a bit easier than his morning run. In total, Mo often runs between 15 and 20 miles a day.

Mo has dinner at around 7 o'clock in the evening. Tania enjoys cooking and prepares a healthy meal of chicken or fish with vegetables or pasta. After a few hours of relaxation, Mo goes to bed at 9.30pm. He needs plenty of sleep to make sure he is ready for another hard day's training the following day.

A touching moment at the London Olympics as Mo gives his daughter Rihanna a hug after his 10,000 metres win.

TOP TIP

'Make sure you eat well the night before a race. Eat loads of carbs like race, pasta or potato. The next day you're going to be running hard so you want to have as much energy as you can.' – Mo Farah

The impact of Mo Farah

From an early age, Mo's natural talent for running was obvious to all who watched him. He won race after race as a schoolboy. But when it came to racing as a senior, Mo struggled to keep up with the world's top runners. He needed to dedicate himself to athletics if he was to be the best.

The turning point in Mo's life came when he saw how African athletes trained. They worked hard, rested and ate simple food. Mo decided he would be like them and each year he travelled to Africa to train alongside them. It meant he had to be away from home for many months of the year. Mo found it hard being apart from his family but it was a sacrifice he knew he had to make.

Mo's victories at the World Championships and the Olympic Games show what can be achieved through determination and hard work. Mo was not prepared to be second best. He did everything in his power to become the greatest long-distance runner in the world.

*Fans cheer as Mo receives a gold medal at the London Olympics. Mo's achievements in athletics have made him a **role model** for many people.*

When Mo arrived in London at the age of eight, he left his life in Somalia behind. But now that he is successful, Mo is trying to make life better for people in the country where he was born. Somalia is very poor and often suffers from **drought**. Mo and Tania have set up a charity called the Mo Farah Foundation which raises money to help children in Somalia with food, water, shelter and medical care.

Mo's next project is to build the Mo Farah Orphanage and Sports Academy in the north of Somalia. He wants to give children the same kind of opportunity he had. Who knows, one of them might turn out to be a champion runner just like Mo.

WOW!

Mo won a £250,000 prize for the Mo Farah Foundation by completing every challenge on the television show 'The Cube'.

At a press conference in 2011, Mo and his wife Tania talk about the plans for the Mo Farah Foundation.

Have you got what it takes to be a champion runner?

1) Would you be prepared to spend months away from home just training and sleeping, as Mo does?
a) Yes. I know you have to make sacrifices if you want to be the best.
b) I could try but I think I would find it hard to be away for months at a time. A few weeks would be better.
c) No, I wouldn't. I like my home comforts too much and I would miss going out with my friends.

2) Do you like energetic activities or would you rather play with a computer or video game?
a) I'd much rather be running around. Sometimes I feel as if I have excess energy to burn.
b) It depends. I do like energetic games but only when I'm in the mood.
c) Give me a computer any day. I find playing on it much more enjoyable than running around.

3) Could you give up fatty foods like burgers and pizza and stick to healthy foods such as chicken and fish?
a) No problem. I know you have to be careful what you eat if you are training as an athlete.
b) I could try, but I might have to cheat occasionally.
c) No way could I could give them up! Chicken and fish sounds really plain and boring.

4) When you are playing sport or a game, how important is it for you to win?
a) Very important. I hate losing and I always try my hardest to win.
b) I enjoy winning, but I don't expect to win all the time. Sometimes it's just nice to take part.
c) I'm not particularly bothered about winning. Some people get far too serious and competitive when they play sport.

5) Could you cope with running long distances in training, even when your body is hurting and you want to stop?
a) Yes. I could put up with the pain because I know it's the only way to improve as a runner.
b) It all depends how my body is feeling. I'd try my best but everyone has their limits.
c) I'm not very good with pain. I think I would just stop if my body was hurting.

RESULTS

Mostly As: You have the right kind of attitude to become a champion runner. Perhaps you should think about joining an athletics club.

Mostly Bs: You have the potential to be a decent runner. The main thing is to enjoy it. Perhaps you will take it more seriously when you're older.

Mostly Cs: It doesn't sound as if you are very sporty but you should try some physical exercise. It's good for health and you might find that you actually enjoy it.

Glossary

agent Someone who represents or acts on behalf of another person, such as an athlete or an actor, in matters of business, e.g. by negotiating the terms of a contract.

altitude Another word for height. Long-distance runners train at high-altitude (over 2,400 metres or 8,000 feet above sea level), where the air contains less oxygen, to increase their fitness and endurance ability.

carbohydrates A group of nutrients in starchy and sugary foods including bread, potatoes and rice, that provide the human body with energy.

civil war A war between opposing groups within the same country.

coaches Training or fitness advisors.

cross-country A type of long-distance running in which athletes compete by racing each other across open country rather than on a road or track.

cryogenic chamber A device inside which athletes can spend a few minutes after training. The inside of the chamber is cooled to incredibly low temperatures. This form of physical therapy is used, in the same way as an ice bath, to provide pain relief and to prevent muscle injury.

decibels Units used to measure the loudness of sounds.

dedicated Committed to a goal and working hard to achieve it.

drought A long period of low rainfall, which can affect the growth of crops and the supply of water for people to drink.

embassy A country's diplomatic building where the ambassador and staff work, usually based in the capital city of a foreign country.

endurance The ability to keep working or exercising for long periods.

form Physical condition or fitness.

gruelling Describes something that is very difficult and tiring to do.

marathon A long-distance running race in which athletes compete over a course measuring 26.2 miles (42.2 kilometres).

professional Someone who is paid for what they do.

protein A group of nutrients in foods including meat, fish, eggs and lentils, that help to keep the human body healthy.

refugee camp A place of shelter for people who have had to leave their homes because of war or as the result of a natural disaster, such as a flood or famine.

role model Someone who is successful in sport or some other field. The way they behave is often copied by others, especially young people.

sports psychologist A professional therapist who specialises in the ways in which the mind can affect performance in sport, e.g. by building confidence, focus and motivation to achieve a goal.

visa An official notification in a passport that gives permission for the passport holder to enter the country issuing the visa.

Index

INSPIRATIONAL LIVES

Contents of new titles in the series

Tom Daley
978 0 7502 7999 4

Diving superstar
Taking the plunge
Conquering fears
Beating the adults
Early setbacks
Back on top
First Olympics
World beater
Darkest days
London looms
Olympic hero
A day in the life of Tom Daley
The impact of Tom Daley
Have you got what it takes
  to be a world-beating diver?

Jessica Ennis
978 0 7502 7998 7

The world's greatest all-rounder
Early potential
A growing medal collection
Senior breakthrough
Injury nightmare
On top of the world
A winning habit
Joy turns to anxiety
Back on track
Golden girl
Honouring a champion
A day in the life of Jessica Ennis
The impact of Jessica Ennis
Have you got what it takes
  to be an Olympic champion?

Mo Farah
978 0 7502 7996 3

Mighty Mo
Growing up in Africa
A new start
Schoolboy champion
Learning his craft
Time to get serious
Tough at the top
Getting faster
On top of the world
Olympic hero
Time to celebrate
A day in the life of Mo Farah
The impact of Mo Farah
Have you got what it takes
  to be a champion runner?

Ellie Simmonds
978 0 7502 7800 3

Paralympic glory
Small, that's all
Into the pool
Making sacrifices
In competition
Ellie's first Paralympics
Dealing with fame
In training
Building on Beijing
A day in the life of Ellie Simmonds
Second time around
After the Games
The impact of Ellie Simmonds
Have you got what it takes
  to be a champion swimmer?

WAYLAND